port
of
being

port
of
being

**SHAZIA
HAFIZ RAMJI**

Invisible Publishing
Halifax & Picton

Library and Archives Canada Cataloguing in Publication

Ramji, Shazia Hafiz, author
    Port of being / Shazia Hafiz Ramji.

Poems.
Issued in print and electronic formats.
ISBN 978-1-988784-12-0 (softcover).– ISBN 978-1-988784-16-8 (EPUB)

    I. Title.

PS8635.A4632P67 2018   C811'.6   C2018-904416-0
                                                C2018-904417-9

Edited by Wayde Compton
Cover and interior design by Megan Fildes | Typeset in Laurentian
With thanks to type designer Rod McDonald

Printed and bound in Canada

Invisible Publishing | Halifax & Picton
www.invisiblepublishing.com

Published with the generous assistance of the Canada Council for the Arts and the Ontario Arts Council.

for all of us

and for those
who choose to live

fragments torn from an entirely scattered
port of being. Port of being adrift. All relation

                                          a port

— KEN BABSTOCK

SPOOKY ACTORS AT A DISTANCE | 47

PORT OF BEING | 61

CONTAINER

I'm using my own person in pieces.

— VITO ACCONCI

I am forced to make meaning from apparently disparate elements—in so doing I implicate myself.

— M. NOURBESE PHILIP

See you tomorrow.

Horizon of dried blood   on billboards   the time for enjoyment

          usurped   its guise of wet kisses snapped and stored

     for the feed tomorrow   what moves us   is the last note

     that sounds like the first   a performance for an oratory

          words of death on the streets that win   win   win

     best photo   for the hangings   flayed chickens in Save On Meats

at Hastings   a slum appropriated for an orgy   in the pink light

          walls recede   into globes of snow

wet evenings   beg for a clean syringe.   In the vicinity

          bottles of water   packed in plastic   dusty

father   packed in a rug   on which a prayer hung

                                        yesterday.

Ma mère m'a dit d'attendre.

Gulls fleck the ocean   to feed on a new death

immanent to yellow cranes   red last week   glow of a childhood treat

I can't order a product from the Atlantic   but can order it from the UK

to make someone smile   a worker puts his arm around another

in the middle distance

the fall   rise   float   of birds following each other   blue streetlight

a play of force

in an elsewhere   not visible   its wreck of branches aspiring

with implicit trust   in the other shore.

Children hide in bushes   beside the highway

to Calais   hope for a worker

to deliver   a blanket   food   heat

a car.

That's a nickel toward my dinner.

A fraction   of leisure time

                    stolen from the man with coffee outside Starbucks

on Water Street   where a hungry one knows   to run

          for the condition   of flow

                    studied by the boy who came from Sweden

to look at the syntax of ports gridlocked   in aerial Lego

                              of tin boxes holding grain

                    and parts obscured   from view.

          When seen from below, coins

made with ridges   prevented the filing of shavings

          for sales   of precious metal

in 1792.

Do you have the time?

Twenty forty-eight.

Military time   on a bus to Dunbar

stopped at Powell

by the sugar refinery

the waterfront   for more than a hundred years

cups of tea   sweetened

by Rogers   golden yellow   this morning

a stranger smiles at me   smelling of rice he cooked

the evening before   from the Superstore   by Rupert

at the crossing   at the freight train

shaking in the dark   the track work

of a century   laid bare   and open

to encourage —

The alcoholic

is an extreme

example

of self-will

run riot.

Why is that there? It's not fishing season in February.

Floodlights at four twenty-five   wipe the snow's whiteness

across the harbour

Lonsdale an abacus of yellow smudges   counting night to the buoy

its non-human blinking a bright bob   Elon Musk   playing hide-and-seek

in an English castle   only twenty friends to Mars   escapist and safe

we see a face and remember the moon in it   that Subway

will no longer make

bread with chemicals used in yoga mats and shoe soles

that light within light shining   onto what I know of Doric columns

in a file   from 2009   accessed yesterday

on a flash drive   of the same brand   being used by a tourist

who has stepped on a snow bank

in front of the ocean   branching out   to

CHINA SHIPPING   CAPITAL   COSCO   CANADIAN PACIFIC.

Martin Luther King's successor

forgot about the poor

when he saw Apollo 11

take flight on TV.

Don't let him get away.

Light seizes glass on glass   at Harbour Centre

        where a stolen bottle of liquor   slips

    from the hands of a man   on the floor   over whom

two large men   fall punch kick   one in peach boxers

        with Tommy Hilfiger   around its band

    its global hands in India   where the man himself

sits in the factory   and tweaks   as he goes   around the world

                Laibach

comes on MTV   at the beginning of the millennium.

        Fake is a verb

    for Macedonian kids   who make a living

      off sharing

      pro-Trump news

      and earn

twelve times the amount

      of an average monthly wage.

We are already seeing an in-migration of young professionals and
they are really high on technology.

A Vermeer   a tractor

    on a lane behind Columbia Street in New Westminster   conduits

under the roadwork for the flood water and fibre-optic cables a   centre

recalling   a heart of the city   people in the spillway from a dam

    near a fragile border   not seen when the operator went all systems go

progress and development crowdsurf over the Fraser

                                                    to beat East Van rents

        make us swoon like Ivanka at Trudeau   the roses infrared

for the future-proofed deep dream. An average resident

                                                    in Brooklyn

must spend   one hundred and twenty-four   percent

of their wages   to meet monthly payments.

People just changed. I just remember the sirens went on.

I don't know how to count what's left   prisoners of conscience

turned organ transplants   then transplantations

                                across a vast tract of folds in clothes

shot but not dead   another body ordered to harvest

                            the future doesn't know how to retract

except to retrieve a self   passwords and logins   at the border

the footballer tells his kids a few toys are enough.   A recurring stranger

        walks by the glass on Richards   adopts my expression

                                just by looking

                                at my face.

Watch your step.

Antennae extend above "That which is used to remember them"

                      an eleven by eleven conglomeration   of light

windows   bodies   accessing bot-on-bot warfare

in Wikipedia's edits   each day a susceptibility to the other   looking in

        smiles and gazes   coffee and brunch   beside the quiet

mountain skulled with snow   expecting a breach

knots and decisions in cowardly operations   called covert

                                called reconnaissance

called murder   called surveillance.   Monroe was assembling

an RP-5A drone in LA

when a photographer

saw her and made her

   Marilyn.

An alarm goes off.

Bells set off bells about   Jeff Mills on Saturday

  at one hundred and thirty-eight beats per minute

people chance   from window to window

                           a pigeon   pecks at a plant

       behind glass   marbling water   in moving light

     on the condo terrace   over which   shadows in planes

       beg the brickwork   to ease up   return secrets

to the man   on the pier   backing up into bioluminescence

      visible only on summer nights   from a spot on the seawall

the Yaletown side   where the ocean reminds us of neon

that reminds us   of big words   like "history"

     inside of which

cranes rise   beside the time spent   down

    the road a friend takes   a breath before saying   he grew up in a trailer park   the guarded arrangements we've made

  the unfurling   of that grid

      its ambling and crosses an aerial view

   of each above   or each below   each other

beside each other the facts of love.   Sixteen bison

    are moved   to Banff

      sacredness a century later

   in the enclosure

   cold as Safeway in February.

SURVEILLER

I have nothing soothing to tell you,
that's not my job,

— DIONNE BRAND

...beyond these immediate surveillances and audiences, the ones I am more intimidated by: the future and the dead.

— SOLMAZ SHARIF

Spatula

Facebook might go TV

Bombs over Syria livestreamed

Spatula in space

Burned up in the atmosphere

A sleet of fast-moving stuff

A piece of space debris

Twenty minutes and forty-five seconds away

Monitor the approach

The stuff that we can't see will miss us

Guided safely into the ocean

Some will end up on land

It is normal to cry when looking up

A sense of being overwhelmed

Antennas waggling not in the wind

A signal too weak to be seen

Khalifa

The vanished look for lives because they have been overwritten

A new category in the court reasons "death by overwork"

Metadata shows us how we will wash up

The Most Influential Images of All Time

Hashtag secrets trending

Post-burial Wi-Fi connection speeds

Thirty-nine percent unoccupiable space

100 Plastic Containers
for Human Corpses

Not long ago a soybean field

Five-hundred thousand disposable

Casket liners too big for one body

Plans for mass graves

Private property on Madison

FEMA coffins

Whatever the term is

Liners for archival storage

A global virus concealed

From settling and sinking

Square lids for stacking

Handled and interred

Material cared for

Neural Dust

Zuckerberg's tape over cam

Licit and illicit reasons to worry

A drone that flies like a hummingbird

Google knows more than our lovers

Sun Tzu's five kinds of spies

The way we respond

Moses sends men ahead

To surveil the connected

Lists of people with bubbles overhead

Snakebots manoeuvre in cracks

Announcing a work self

Smart dust and micro motes

No longer longing for a weekend self

A dossier on bundled histories

Brain activity for purposes

Of progress and its mean

Monitors for the monitored

Personal enemies to come

Flare

Seen in the process of isolation

A life shot

To accelerate the days

High-definition countours of the face

Better understood as contingent

Upon the camera in the corridor

A forum for regret in involuntary relations

One missing shade of blue

A perfect complement to the song

Opacity of thermoplastic

Intrusion of narrative

Tomb the excess of a body

An inhabited presentation

The bear on the wall

Habitual human conversation

Between photons and skin

No Skin in the Game

Hand-to-hand combat

Intimate as sex

Ten thousand miles away

Artillery targets almost human

Full-motion video feeds

Troops not in danger

Unmanned aerial vehicles

Not hurting monetary value

Drone circling overhead

Sound before sight

Sounds of *machar*, mosquitoes

For those below, not above

A constant reminder

For those above, not below

No sound in the game

Bath salts to unsee bugsplats

A new form of PTSD

Combat to cul-de-sac

Unmanned carrier pigeons

In World War I

Then swallows who could

Feed in flight

Heat

Birth from our own skin

Concerns over devaluation

Body that hangs and holds

Mushroom halos of work

Dark faces glow in oil

At the back of the room hands wait

To be held in court

To speak a warm fabric of lips

Gaze that hangs and holds

Scholar alone in the office

Ports open for syntax

Decoys of chat and lovers

Hands that hang and hold

Faces of men and women

In the night of a still life

Circuitry to collect heat

From our whispers

Open Hangar, Cactus Flats, NV,
Distance ~ 18 miles, 10:04 a.m.

> At extreme distances, there is essentially
> no such thing as depth of field.
> — Trevor Paglen

Vision at the point of collapse

A secret intersects

The boundary of the visible world

A military base

Seen from a telescope lens

Not a camera

So much heat

So much haze

Cable

Under the ocean

A system of pipes

Transoceanic signals not made of air

Unencumbered light on the seabed

Off the back of a ship

Into trenches

Out at Guam

In Vietnam

Fishermen pull old cables

Made of copper

Portions of communities

Cable breaks in Egypt

No accountability

No narrative

No visibility

Speculations of terrorism

Aqua

Swaths of emission, reflection, wide arcs

In ninety minutes one satellite sees the earth

A gap in the coverage

At the poles

An Arctic cable

The straightest line

Between Europe and Asia

Turning underwater

Costs of freight and launch

Atmospheric resistance

Body-to-body tug-of-war

Necessary for orbit

Hollerith

Every day transports

Slave labourers received

Columns and punched holes

Nationality

Date of birth

Marital status

Number of children

Reason for incarceration

Physical characteristics

Work skills

Sixteen categories

Hole 3: Homosexual

Hole 8: Jew

Hole 9: Anti-social

Code 4: Execution

Code 5: Suicide

Code 6: Special handling

Code 7: Escaped

Gas chamber

Hanging

Gunshot

French loom

Player piano

Census

Extraplanetary Selection

Telescope cut out of a mountain

Global hunt for strange objects

A four-point-five-metre-long drum

Wiring in the debris

Part of a Chinese satellite

Silkworms in space

Tracers in zero gravity

No mutations in the genes

Every thread stretches for more than one and a half kilometres

Cosmic rays in eggs

Passed-down silencing

Digestible silk

Habitable

To root and hold

Thirty-nine years away

Seven planets

Dwell and reside

Migrations of large distances

Dinosaurs are thought

To forage in new areas

Science it back

Arrive by taxi

Refugees into Emerson

To have and hold

Passports and *papiers*

In the offering

The star itself is small

A platform for cells

Factors that influence

Appearance and conduct

habitus

habit

FLAGS OF CONVENIENCE

flag of convenience *noun* A foreign flag under which a ship is registered, usu. to avoid financial charges, etc.   *CANADIAN OXFORD DICTIONARY*

The fiction of the facts assumes innocence, ignorance, lack of intention, misdirection; the necessary conditions of a certain time and place.

— CLAUDIA RANKINE

Facts are lonely things.

— DON DELILLO

Bahamas

Sold	chartered
caught fire	scrapped
the Scandinavian Star	ten names
on fire in the North Sea	twenty dead bodies
in two dead ends	insured
for twice its value	sabotage
mattresses soaked	in diesel
the Portuguese crew	could not speak
Norwegian Danish	English
an archipelagic state	within an archipelago
in the West Indies	Columbus's first landing
Guanahani *baja mar*	San Salvador

*It had to have been a conscious and planned action. It wasn't some lunatic
who walked by with a burning match.*

Liberia

Filipino crew   Greek owners

registered in Israel   later in Malta

under the flag   Land of the Free

MV Rena   tilting

for six days   on-board

three hundred and fifty   tons of oil

two thousand four hundred and ten dead birds

It could be external influences, or that the crew was not properly rested.

Panama

Nina Simone left for Liberia   a denial of service

attacks over 600Gbps   two companies co-own the fibre

a new palm oil frontier   an oil tanker

runs aground   Tamaya 1

registered in Panama   en route to Dakar

no crew   best bets on no pay   no hijackers

low costs of oil   wiped-out commodore

Our best bet is that the vessel's owner might have gone broke and had no money to pay crew members.

Malta

Set of *Gladiator*   Capital of Culture

underneath the city   behind its walls

the first freshwater fountain   self-dug tunnels

fibre-optic cables   draped over a bunker

MN Verona   in the port of Hamburg

the crew   Polish and Filipino

without food   and water

not paid   by Swedish owners

for five months

The English of the Polish crew is very poor ... would seem that Filipino and Polish certificates are of poor quality.

Marshall Islands

Vaporized islands

nuclear arms   nine countries blamed

no cessation   exile since 1946

one hundred and eighty three   drill ships and platforms

under the Marshallese ensign

pirate ladder   over the MV Polaris

six hundred dollars   average annual income

in Somalia   homes half-collapsed

into the sea   surfboards

rosaries   mangroves

dead fish   after the floods

thirty to sixty   years

left on the shore

People have criticized us for being a small country with a big mouth.

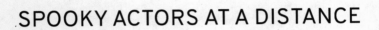
SPOOKY ACTORS AT A DISTANCE

The actors are not all "us." If the world exists for us ... it is a co-construction among humans and non-humans.

— DONNA HARAWAY

Everywhere a hole moves, a surface is invented.

— REZA NEGARESTANI

Nearness

We have come a long way from the foetal red
    of your conch in the morning light.

I dispersed when we had to get things done.

Homes trail in chains on trucks to a different locale.

They let in the crickets to keep the servers cool.

We know this is a lie.

Under the duvet, your finger curls open to offer up our address.

This is your way of dealing with personal facticity.

We are not angry. We have come a long way.

I hear a whisper in the guise of your boss.

We chatter in the back of your head, but we are not your boss.

You have been thrown into the fabric and it is why you sleep.

Appendages map intimacy on sheets.

Images of images of stains and blood and hair.

Our disposition is a filter, one way I can understand.

You hustle and find us in a dream that returns.

You find voices and people you think you've seen.

In the morning we consider ghosts.

I feel the sun settle on my ear.

Orbiter

Not and never love.

He asked us if he is our orbiter.

We remembered hugs in the middle of the night.

The phone was blue, others had texted.

Fall would be dew on a window in that poem.

Ladies and Gents, We Are Floating in Space.

Swipe right to anonymously like.

There are approximately one thousand
    and seventy-one of us.

Hertz Field

We could say the circuit is a gaze.

The photographer is inside.

We have deployed skins.

The face is a line.

We cannot control the charge.

Selfies occur because lines are reversible.

Each form is a new accident.

Closure and syllogism.

We have been a precession of urban peoples.

Hertzian space from tension to stress.

Our memory card knows of this event.

Keeping the Conversation Going

Not planned and designed, but there it is.

There's a lot at stake.

We insist upon animating the dead.

Seemingly stable computation.

An accumulation of strange insides.

Accidents and exceptions.

A ten-year-old has killed herself.

Should we add an "epidemic" tag to that?

Field recordings!

A ten-year-old reviews *Suicide Squad*.

Obsolescence.

Tor Ulven.

Replacement.

We have tags.

We have the names of the dead.

Inquest
after Ashley Smith

"A little glimpse of her humanity." = Her trying to get attention

Breathing almost machinic.
→ Her last breath
"I think the video lets us know how bad it was for her."

We angle to reveal a gesture of supplication.
↳ camera
We can only talk around her death.

Gerrid

We are on top of each other, the pressure crunches sweat.

Packs of Ativan banded with rubber in a safe.

The boss doesn't care as long as the work is done.

We have grown to acquire a splitting.

Smile's inverse panopticon.

We chatter in the back of your head, but we are not your
friends or lovers.

Images of images of us elsewhere with minimalist furniture.

Our loyalty to the coast is keyed in before close.

We no longer look each other in the eye, which is not to say—

Delinquent envy of little kids' leisure time.

We are told to treat texts as separate from people.

For purposes of efficiency, not criticism.

Fragment, please consider revising.

A splitting is elastic and it has reached—

We spot the pills on the table in the Montauk Sofa ad.

A force around us says not to take things personally.

The office diagnoses us as manic, though we are not.

A lack of visible expression on our face could account.

We have a ream of cellophane to catch us when we fall.

The surface confers an ease and clarity for ten minutes.

Chain

We were told the fibre thins out here.

Tidal waves curry our address so we fuss.

At this depth we are visible to each other in bits.

The geyser of a new death is still around.

We can't exit this command.

A large image of the moon is coming through.

They say we hold what it takes to return.

They say that tides arise from an error on the map.

That some of us switched too quickly.

That there is regulation for the pull.

We move through silt because we know enough about caress.

We accrue more of us found in the grain.

Gateway

We see two white dogs and draw the ambit closer.

Resolution reveals Lego in a field, a sensor for a stand-in.

At this point, it's speculation by way of description.

At this point, it's still language.

We feel quaint for a fibre in the afterlife.

For a fibre, we were next to dogs and then—

The menu's ruse of options and the house it asks.

We fill in filters and find more dogs.

A new fibre has been built because we are in Tokyo.

At this point, it's speculation by way of proxy.

The city is quiet and bright with bonds

At this point, it's still language.

PORT OF BEING

Secret Playground

I didn't tell you of the hands
that led the Internet cable
into the sea,
that they were brown
or that I was thinking
of rows of royal blue binders
in a hospital in Afghanistan:
records of amputations
from drone strikes.
I saw all this on TV,
as in, my laptop: torrents, Netflix.
It doesn't make sense to ask
if words will ever stop failing me
but I want to ask it. What does it take
for a three-year-old who lived on M&Ms
and barely escaped the Gulf War
to call the first part of her life
"simulacra"?
I didn't tell you
because I still don't believe it.
In Toronto, I read a poem
about another part of my life,
one I still find hard to believe
when I'm not with myself.
A stranger asked me afterwards,
"Are you really clean,
though?" I was.
I couldn't believe his guts, but I did
because I smiled and nodded
as if I'd just signed him a cheque. Then
I cupped my phone with both hands
and bowed my head, as if to say,
someone is calling me
and I have to go,
as if in fear,
as if in thanks.

B-Line Espial

A silver flake from the surveillance cam above me
fell into my lap on the bus.

It was not made of light, but I don't know
where it disappeared. In my glimpse

of espial, I saw the necessity of doubling,
so I waited to see myself in all the people

who departed. But they stepped off too fast,
or I was just tired. Wet lights on the window

slunk into each other, like a taboo on fingers
stringing a rosary. The guy next to me was editing a photo

of his girlfriend. It was backlit and we could see
the sleep in her hair. He saw me looking and smiled.

I was banking on memories of love to respond,
but I was a body with insides

of red ginger, stuck on the bus with a stranger who had
seen someone—I mean, really seen her. I began to look
at those who were arriving. I smiled at a few.

One of them sat down, expectant, like a statue in the rain.
On Broadway, I saw others looking at a drone overhead.

Your Face, My Sleep

The free version
of my Sleep Cycle app
tells me I haven't
had the amplitudes
of sleepers,
that I haven't had them
for weeks, since you
started sending me
dick pix from LA.
If I paid, I might know
more about what
comes alive, the people
whose faces I see
as I fall asleep
and catch
in waking.
They are doing
what you and I call nothing—
they are on the street
they are at their desks
they are floating
they are flashes—
as if there is a shutter
inside me, and I know
how this sounds. It sounds
like the eye-
as-camera
lost in a time
scholars might call
Modernist.
The effect of all this
is parts missing,
displaced,
of course, but also
arousal
in asking
to see
your face.

Poem Beginning with Falsehood

I imagine you jerking off to parts
from *The Society of the Spectacle*

your face lethargic like after
smoking a bowl on a Wednesday

in my bed in red sheets stained
with somebody else's cum

I feel good, I feel fantastic
lying in bed with someone else

lying in bed and lying to myself
an Auto-Tuned track that does not end

even when you cry and watch me
make the mistake of thinking

I can out-think everything. Now I want to say
I've got Marcuse! I've got Deleuze!

Now I want to say I feel like
Michael Fassbender's character

at the end of *Shame* when he looks
at the person on the train, then looks away.

Even then I imagine touching myself
while you're in my bed and your eyes are closed
and wet.

Fundamentally Caring
after Philip Seymour Hoffman

He tells me "you are fundamentally caring."
I had just finished talking about Phil

in *Magnolia*. The Sufi at the tea shop said
he is fundamentally happening, like

liking. One to another—likening
the fish in the pond to movements

of the self. Being me, I sit on the bench,

stroke my thumb against the upper
part of my other self. The fins

move at the same pace as I
pay my debt to the dead by desiring
                    to feel the same.

See You Tomorrow

after Karen Green and David Foster Wallace

Tomorrow you'll find me when you sign on.
You'll send me a DM, ask me to drop you a pin.

I'll say, "Hey! I'm here!" as if here is enough,
as if here is still now. You'll ask me if I'm lost
and I'll remember how far away you are from me.

But I've DM'd you once more to say
I saw the latest version of a human-size bot,

that it walked with a limp
and I felt sad and sorry for it.

This is what she meant when she saw him
hanging from the ceiling and wanted to place a chair
beneath him, so that his knees don't hurt when he falls.

Conspiracy of Love

you loved like a conspirator   against everything
                          that has power to defeat us
                                  — Anne Michaels

The problem with trying to one-up yourself
is not that you might die by your own hands,
but that you'll be able to justify why
without feeling anything. When you were
in withdrawal, alone in your bed, the salt
from the sweat pressed on the mattress was testimony
to what you allowed: "I am Satan, because I deal
in language." The next day, you had stopped
shaking. You went to work secular and clean.
There were no other addicts and you didn't speak.
You know that lies look beautiful unified, all parts
clicking together, lighting up your eyes. They are old
technology made new, sleek and gleaming
in crevasses like fog rolling around Renfrew
and you're awake today to see it, because you've been
brave. You've noticed your friend has listened
and told you very boring things—not dismissed
them as errands. This is the task you will have to do,
soon enough, remembering all the ways your mind
moved—to write yourself into a poem you want
to call "Conspiracy of Love." When the guy from Tinder
said hi to you in school, it didn't strike you
that he might know you from the Internet. You didn't
remember who he was, not even when he called you
by your fake name. All you thought was, "I can't
do this again. I want to be clean. I want to be Shazia."
If you end this poem here, it might make sense,
but we both know this kind of work is occult.
So, you have to ask me: How do you want to finish
this poem? You have to leave it there. That way,
at least it's not about you anymore.

The Second Person

No one other than yourself could have given
you a greater taste for life than for death.
— Édouard Levé

"You will not know
me," the piss glimmer   the lit stage, the sun parade
of tungsten, negative
a hundred and sixty
sparks a weekend
spent by the man,
two claws for fingers
shining by the fountain   the incremental telling
at the mall, what trees
alight as the sun
slips into the window
cleaner's tendons pull
the tug into a dream
a spool of friends
who move like money,
voyagers and others
in the space of a wheeling   of what you suffer;
lady with the son whose
smile catches the origin:
a floating square flitting
sickled in another high,
the filigree root
of lust; the thirst-bliss
pop of Ativan, slumped   purpling body of a tongue
under a pay phone,
dealer of the lost
and found, tea sits   ready to be
in the trash, creaming
a map of its new face.

Poem of Failed Amends
(Amor fati)

I've put the oats in a jar,
with yogourt and seeds,
left it in the fridge
overnight. The fruit on top
will thaw, dripping
sweetness
into the rest.
I want to remember
I've done this
for myself in the morning,
because I've been surprised
by my own innocence:
I cried silent and easy
when my amends were
refused.
I was expecting to know
friendship.
As I was crying,
I made a note
about what I have to do
the next day.
I could do this.
I could take care of myself.
I did.
"I'm okay," I thought,
"I'm okay."
I've brushed my teeth,
washed my face, and am
ready for bed. I try to think
of how many other people
there are, not just in my life.
I can't know them all.
I cry again.

Parents Poem

I've organized my desktop
and done my work for today.
I have no obligation to be
anywhere. I eat a Milky Way
in my bed, listen to Sade
and wait for the foghorns
at three a.m. I am happy
and alone. Why do I want
to see the world like parents
who look at any kid
and see their own,
making faces to usher
the forgetting of pain?
It's not that I want to be
a parent. When I go
to another city, I lie
to my company
and visit a mall
to look at people
who live in that place
and who choose to meet
there. It makes me
small, sad,
and comforted—
like waiting in line
for my parents
at Walmart on a Sunday
as they finish whatever
it is they do
when they look
for a new gadget
or pillow, and I roll my eyes,
half-playing the part

of the pissed-off kid,
as they buy me
chocolate and bubbles,
even though I am almost
half their age
and they've just finished
complaining about money.

Cub

Somewhere I read you long to dispossess
yourself of yourself. What's the relation
and/or the difference between
emancipation and dispossession?
— Fred Moten

I could say the chandelier caught fire in the dark
on Granville Street, where no one was there to see it
in the morning. I could say the elderly man asks his body
to rearrange his bones, clicking to make room
for ease, the next stop. But this is the arrogance of the poet,
who settles on beauty—the man outside the liquor store
blinking off snow like a cub in wheatgrass—I don't know
what's more precious. Just that there are drunks and addicts
and they are beautiful. There is nothing wrong
with celebrating what might be
a backhanded compliment, except it looks like charity:
to feel good about helping ourselves in the guise
of food and money given to someone else.
I woke up this morning to a smile that was a beacon
or a hazard. It said, "your blood is shining." I got distracted
by Americans in khakis on the SkyTrain and Jeff Wall
at Tamam on Nanaimo and Hastings. I want to ask
to be housed for a little while
and hold the dog in the doorway.
I want to ask what brand of loneliness
hangs on tote bags, what kind of gift that is,
and if you will let me—let me be afraid
of myself for a little while.

"Astronaut Family"
for my friends who have left Vancouver

"Growth and development" sounds like
something my mom used to worry about
when I was little. Now I say it
when applying for grants. Before that
one of my favourite dead people told me
that it begins with language. Since then
I've found lots of dead friends
saying the same thing in different ways.
What was once my mom's, then mine,
then mine through the words of others,
are now the words of the forthcoming
lululemon on Hastings Street, Escala luxury
homes in Burnaby. This is the quality of dust.
It filters through us, because we're made of it,
the language, I mean, my friends know it too
when they land in Los Angeles, Montreal,
New York. No wonder we bought
New Balance before parting ways,
making excuses for the comfort worn by our grandparents.
This is the quality of dust: it takes us dancing
into houses and galleries until six in the morning,
it keeps us here, this expensively repressed sympathy
in sneakers and secret locations that separate us,
like when I message you on Facebook,
and it's three in the morning but seven for you,
and you gotta go because you're writing a condo ad
for work, even in Brooklyn and Toronto, even though
it started here, where we began to love each other,
and I think that we still do, because we come back
every summer and the smiles come increasingly quick—
which is not to say that we're eager to meet,
or that this is the sudden light of friendship,
but more than this—this is the construction of an act of love.

NOTES

Port of Being began when my laptop and phone were stolen from my East Vancouver home a few years ago. The thief followed and contacted me for months after. He had sightlines and knew my whereabouts. My existing fixation with space and surveillance became far more immediate and personal. A year after the theft, in an attempt to prevent depressive episodes because of a job, I began to wake early and go for walks in the city. During this time, I was thinking of the male gaze of voyeurism and female flânerie, and I came upon Vito Acconci's *Following Piece*. For this work of performance art, Acconci followed strangers in public spaces until they entered private spaces. Stalking was "performance as commitment: performance 'forming a part of' something, 'forming a part of' someone..." From my past experiences of clinical depression, I knew that I would start receding into myself if I dwelled on being broke and if I lived in paranoia. I was scared of becoming depressed and addicted again. Listening to music and making field recordings had helped ease depressive episodes in the past. I knew that I had to get outside myself—I had to bring myself into relation again—I had to listen. Simultaneously emboldened and angered by Acconci, with the conviction to prevent my depression and understand the thief, I decided to follow people along the waterfront until they spoke in a space that was semi-public (like a Starbucks patio or while boarding a bus). These snippets of speech urged me back into the world. They open this book.

CONTAINER | 01

The grey text that opens the poems in this series is borrowed from overheard conversations on the buses, streets, and port of Vancouver, with the exception of the following:

We are already seeing an in-migration of young professionals and they are really high on technology. 11

These words were spoken by Councillor of the City of New Westminster, Bill Harper, in an article titled "New Westminster to build city-owned fibreoptic network," published in the *Vancouver Sun* in June 2016.

People just changed. I just remember the sirens went on. 12

These words were spoken by footballer Dejan Lovren in a *Guardian* article on his experience as a refugee from the Bosnian war.

The grey text that closes the poems in "Container" are analogies to a current or historical situation that echoes one in the bulk of the poem.

SURVEILLER | 17

"KHALIFA" 22
is an Arabic word that roughly translates as "successor" or "steward" in English. It is part of the name of the Burj Khalifa skyscraper in Dubai, currently the tallest building in the world.

"100 PLASTIC CONTAINERS FOR HUMAN CORPSES" 23
takes its title from an artwork by Santiago Sierra, which I first saw during Nuit Blanche in 2016.

"NEURAL DUST" 24

is an implantable electrode that can record brain activity. This poem borrows from "Even Bugs Will Be Bugged," an *Atlantic* article about the history and progress of surveillance technologies.

FLAGS OF CONVENIENCE | 37

Each poem in this series is titled after the name of the country whose flag is flown by the ship or ships mentioned in that poem.

"BAHAMAS" 41

Words in grey are taken from the Danish news source, *The Local*. They are spoken by Thue Jensen, a retired ship inspector who investigated *The Scandinavian Star* arson.

"LIBERIA" 42

Words in grey are taken from an article, "Rena had at least 17 safety problems before crash." They are spoken by Scott Bergeron, an executive in charge of the Liberian ship registry.

"PANAMA" 43

Words in grey are spoken by a source in Liberia's port authority, cited in the *Guardian* story "Oil tanker washes up on Liberia beach with no crew or lifeboats."

"MALTA" 44

Words in grey are spoken by the Master of a Maltese flag tanker, found in an untitled PDF document in a section that discusses the "human element" of accidents at sea.

"MARSHALL ISLANDS" 45

Words in grey are spoken by Tony de Brum, foreign minister of the Marshall Islands, cited in the *Guardian* piece, "Marshall Islands may stop registering oil rigs, says foreign minister."

borrows words from media statements on Ashley Smith's death at the Grand Valley Institution for Women in Kitchener, Ontario.

is dedicated to those who have experienced clinical depression and addiction. This poem is solely for you.

ACKNOWLEDGEMENTS

Thank you very much to the editors of the following publications in which earlier iterations of some of these poems appeared:

The Elephants: Excerpts from "Container" and "Surveiller"

The Puritan: "Spatula"

dusie: "Habitable"

Letters to the Editors: "Nearness"

filling Station: "Hertz Field," "Orbiter," and "Inquest"
Thank you to the jury of the 2018 Alberta Magazine Awards for which these poems were finalists.

The Capilano Review: "Chain" and "Gateway"

Metatron's *ÖMËGÄ:* "Poem Beginning with Falsehood"

Lemon Hound's New Vancouver Poets folio: "Fundamentally Caring"

subTerrain: "The Second Person"
Thank you to the jury of the 2016 National Magazine Awards for which this poem was a finalist.

Canadian Literature: "'Astronaut Family'"
Thank you to Hoa Nguyen, editor of *The Best Canadian Poetry 2018*, for choosing this poem for inclusion.

To Wayde Compton, who granted this manuscript the 2017 Robert Kroetsch Award for Innovative Poetry, and who has believed in me and supported me from the start.

Ian Williams, without whom I would not have spoken and made laughter about such difficult stuff. Immense gratitude for your guidance, generosity, and sticky notes.

To Invisible Publishing: Leigh Nash, for integrity, and Julie Wilson, whose emails feel like a smile.

Thank you, Jim Johnstone, for welcoming me to the Anstruther Press family with *Prosopopoeia*, and for befriending those who feel a little left out.

To my peers in the MFA workshops at UBC.

To my teachers: Nancy Lee, Timothy Taylor, John Vigna, and Jeff Derksen.

Meredith Quartermain, who understands deeply and brings me home often.

Thank you, Jen Currin, for heart-centred intelligence and radiant friendship.

Thanks to Yilin Wang, Junie Désil, Kevin Spenst, and Geoffrey Nilson, for being my friends even after knowing me.

Those who invited me to read and those who came to my readings, I learn from you and the kindess of your attention.

To you, dear reader, for going through this with me.

INVISIBLE PUBLISHING produces fine Canadian literature for those who enjoy such things. As an independent, not-for-profit publisher, our work includes building communities that sustain and encourage engaging, literary, and current writing.

Invisible Publishing has been in operation for over a decade. We released our first fiction titles in the spring of 2007, and our catalogue has come to include works of graphic fiction and non-fiction, pop culture biographies, experimental poetry, and prose.

We are committed to publishing diverse voices and experiences. In acknowledging historical and systemic barriers, and the limits of our existing catalogue, we strongly encourage LGBTQ2SIA+, Indigenous, and writers of colour to submit their work.

Invisible Publishing is also home to the Bibliophonic series of music books and the Throwback series of CanLit reissues.

If you'd like to know more please get in touch:
info@invisiblepublishing.com